curiousabout
CAMPING

BY KRISSY EBERTH

AMICUS LEARNING

What are you

curious about?

CHAPTER THREE

3

Going on a Camping Trip

PAGE
14

Curious About is published by Amicus Learning,
an imprint of Amicus
P.O. Box 227
Mankato, MN 56002
www.amicuspublishing.us

Editor: Alissa Thielges
Series Designer: Kathleen Petelinsek
Book Designer: Lori Bye

Library of Congress Cataloging-in-Publication Data
Names: Eberth, Kristin, author.
Title: Curious about camping / by Krissy Eberth.
Description: Mankato, Minnesota: Amicus Learning, 2024.
| Series: Curious about the great outdoors | Includes
bibliographical references and index. | Audience: Ages
5–9 | Audience: Grades 2–3 | Summary: "Questions and
answers give kids the fundamentals of camping, including
what to pack and where to camp. Includes infographics to
support visual learning and back matter to support research
skills, plus a glossary and index"—Provided by publisher.
Identifiers: LCCN 2023009719 (print) | LCCN 2023009720
(ebook) | ISBN 9781645496571 (library binding) | ISBN
9781681529462 (paperback) | ISBN 9781645496830 (pdf)
Subjects: LCSH: Camping—Juvenile literature.
Classification: LCC GV191.7 .E24 2024 (print) | LCC
GV191.7 (ebook) | DDC 796.54—dc23/eng/20230313
LC record available at https://lccn.loc.gov/2023009719
LC ebook record available at https://lccn.loc.gov/2023009720

Image credits: Getty/Oxana Denezhkina, 8, Stephen Swintek,
cover, 1, Thomas Barwick, 10, Yagi-Studio, 9; Krissy Eberth,
14–15; Shutterstock/Air Images, 4–5, anatoliy_gleb, 6, Blueee77,
13, Felipe Sanchez, 13, jaboo2foto, 2, 13 (tent), Javier Cruz
Acosta, 11, Jesse Seniunas, 12, KPixMining, 16, mariakray,
20–21, minizen, 22, 23, New Africa, 17, Pikoso.kz, 13,
Rexjaymes, 13, Soloviova Liudmyla, 18–19, VectorMine, 7

Printed in China

What should I wear camping?

DID YOU KNOW?
Quick-drying or wicking clothes are best. Cotton and denim stay wet for a long time. They can make you cold.

First, check the weather. If it's hot, wear shorts and a T-shirt. Bring a rain jacket in case it rains. If it's cold, wear long pants and a sweatshirt. Mornings can be chilly. You might need a coat, mittens, and a hat. Hiking boots protect your feet from sharp rocks. Closed-toe sandals protect your toes in the water.

Many people fish while camping in the summer.

The night sky looks clearer when camping.

What if I'm afraid of the dark?

TYPES OF CAMPFIRES

Log Cabin

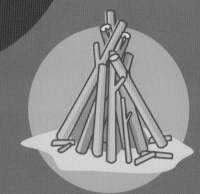

Tepee

Star

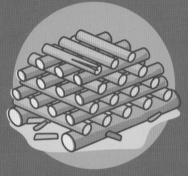

Pyramid

That's okay. You can learn to love the dark. Building a fire and telling stories is fun at night. You can use a flashlight or headlamp to see. Bring a special blanket or stuffed animal to help with your fear.

What gear will I need?

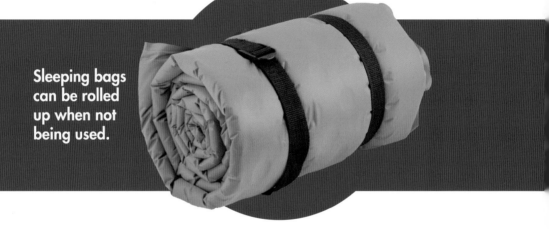

Sleeping bags can be rolled up when not being used.

You will need a sleeping bag, tent, pad, and pillow for sleeping. You also need utensils, pots, and dishes for cooking and eating. Put your gear in a backpack or plastic bin. That makes it easier to carry. Don't forget sunscreen!

A tent keeps you safe from bugs and rain.

rain fly

poles

tent body

mesh door

guy lines

tent stakes

CHAPTER TWO

Where can I go camping?

DID YOU KNOW?
Backcountry camping is done in the wilderness. You must hike to your spot.

Backcountry campers carry everything they need to their spot.

You can start in your backyard! That's a good place to practice. National and state parks have great campsites. Some places have toilets, showers, and even a pool! Others are more **rustic**. They don't have running water. **Reserve** a campsite that fits your interests.

Campgrounds have many sites to choose from.

Do I have to sleep outdoors?

Cabins can be a relaxing place to be in nature.

No. Not everyone camps in a tent. Some people have **RV**s or campers. These are like houses on wheels with beds and even electricity. People drive or pull them behind their vehicles. Some people stay in a cabin or **yurt**.

TENT

YURT

POP UP CAMPER

FIFTH WHEEL RV

MOTORHOME

What can I do when I'm camping?

There's so much to do! Hiking, biking, and swimming are all fun. Some campers rock climb, fish, or go **birding**. You can explore the area and look for animals. If it rains, you can play cards or a board game. Canoeing and kayaking are also great to try!

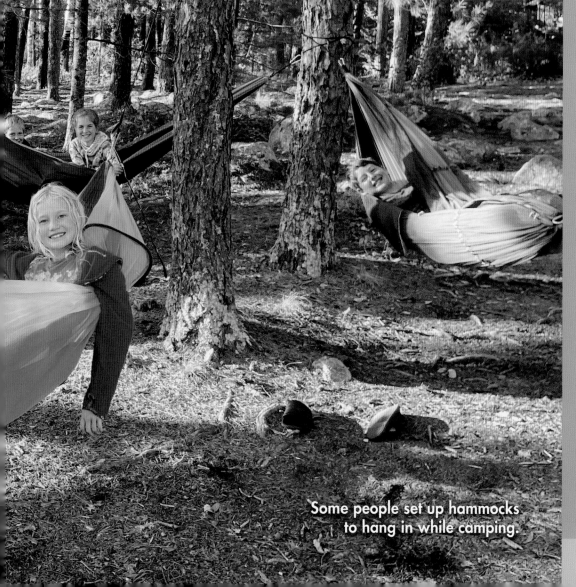

Some people set up hammocks to hang in while camping.

Deer ticks can carry diseases.

Are there bugs?

Yes. There can be lots of bugs depending on where you camp. Bring bug spray! Every evening, check your body for **ticks**. Long pants, socks, and long sleeves can prevent bug bites. If you do get an itchy bite, put on **calamine lotion**.

Put on bug spray before a hike to avoid bug bites.

Roasted marshmallows are a classic camping food.

What do I eat?

DID YOU KNOW?
S'mores were invented
in 1927.

You bring all your own food. Try to pick easy
things to make. Hot dogs on a stick and oatmeal
are good choices. You can cook them over a
fire. Pack lots of snacks, like trail mix. Being
active outside makes you hungry. Don't forget
the s'mores! They make a tasty campfire treat.

What if I have to go to the bathroom?

Campgrounds have bathrooms. You just walk a short distance to the bath house. Some RVs have bathrooms inside! Rustic campsites have **pit toilets**. Bring hand sanitizer to clean your hands.

Pit toilets can be found near hiking trails and rustic campsites.

ASK MORE QUESTIONS

What can I cook over a campfire?

Can you go camping in the winter?

Try a BIG QUESTION:
How does camping affect the environment?

SEARCH FOR ANSWERS

Search the library catalog or the Internet.
A librarian, teacher, or parent can help you.

Using Keywords
Find the looking glass.

Keywords are the most important words in your question.

?

If you want to know about:

- what to cook over a fire, type: CAMPFIRE RECIPES

- camping in the winter, type: WINTER CAMPING

FIND GOOD SOURCES

Are the sources reliable?

Some sources are better than others. An adult can help you. Here are some good, safe sources.

Books

Go Camping
by Heather Bode, 2023.

Camping
by Lisa Owings, 2023.

Internet Sites

Smokey for Kids
https://smokeybear.com/en/prevention-how-tos/campfire-safety/how-to-build-your-campfire
Smokey the Bear teaches kids (and adults) how to safely make and put out a fire.

U.S. National Park Service | How to Camp
https://www.nps.gov/subjects/camping/how-to-camp.htm
The U.S. National Park Service is in charge of all national parks. Here you will find all sorts of camping advice, from planning to activities.

Every effort has been made to ensure that these websites are appropriate for children. However, because of the nature of the Internet, it is impossible to guarantee that these sites will remain active indefinitely or that their contents will not be altered.

SHARE AND TAKE ACTION

Camp in your backyard!

Ask an adult to help you set up a tent.

Plan a visit to a state park.

How many days will you stay? How much food and supplies will you need to bring?

Become a Junior Ranger!

Most national parks have a program. You can complete activities at home and receive a patch and certificate when you visit a national park.

GLOSSARY

birding To watch birds in the wild.

calamine lotion A creamy medicine that you spread over the skin to relieve itchiness.

pit toilet A type of toilet that collects human waste in a hole in the ground.

reserve To make arrangements to use or have something at a later time.

rustic A simple campsite that does not have water or modern bathrooms.

RV Recreational vehicle; a large vehicle with a bed, bathroom, and kitchen that is used during travel.

tick A small insect that drinks the blood of animals and people.

yurt A round tent covered by animal skins that can be taken down to move.

wick away A fabric that moves sweat away from the skin.

INDEX

About the Author

Krissy Eberth loves adventure, especially camping with her husband and two daughters. When away from her writing desk, she can be found skiing, hiking, or biking the trails of northern Minnesota.

Hechos increíbles, REPUGNANTES e insólitos de las MOMIAS

Stephanie Bearce

BLACK RABBIT BOOKS

Hi Jinx es una publicación de Black Rabbit Books
P.O. Box 227, Mankato, Minnesota, 56002
www.blackrabbitbooks.com
Copyright © 2024 Black Rabbit Books

Alissa Thielges, editora; Michael Sellner,
diseñador del interior y investigación fotográfica

Información del catálogo de publicaciones de la biblioteca del
congreso
Names: Bearce, Stephanie, author.
Title: Hechos increíbles, repugnantes e insólitos de las momias /
Stephanie Bearce.
Other titles: Awesome, disgusting, unusual facts about
mummies. Spanish Description: Mankato, Minnesota:
Black Rabbit Books, 2024. |
Series: Cosas asquerosas e increíbles de la historia |
Includes index. | Audience: Ages 8–12 | Audience: Grades 4–6 |
Summary: "Gross and weird facts about mummies will grab
struggling and reluctant readers' attention as they learn about
different types of mummification and famous mummies, such
as King Tut, in this Spanish translation."—Provided by publisher.
Identifiers: LCCN 2023023280 (print) | LCCN 2023023281
(ebook) | ISBN 9781623109714 (library binding) |
ISBN 9781644666333
(paperback) | ISBN 9781623109776 (ebook)
Subjects: LCSH: Mummies—Egypt—Juvenile literature.
Classification: LCC DT62.M7 B3418 2024 (print) | LCC DT62.M7
(ebook) | DDC 932—dc23/eng/20230602
LC record available at https://lccn.loc.gov/2023023280
LC ebook record available at https://lccn.loc.gov/2023023281

Impreso en China

Créditos de las imágenes
AgeFototock: M Lohmann 12–13; Alamy: Chronicle 7
(bkgd), Dennis Cox 19, Gerhard Zwerger-Schoner 16 (bl),
MediaWorldImages 16 (br), Michele Burgess 11; Flickr: Michael
Thirnbeck 13; Getty: AFP 16 (t), 20, Alexis DUCLOS 8 (b), Apic 15,
Bettmann cover; Michele's Musings on Mummies: Michelle Brittany
8 (m); Science Source: Carlos Munoz-Yage 8 (t); Shutterstock: Albert
Ziganshin 5, Alexander_P 7 (brain), Framalicious 4, ilolab cover,
1, 8 (bkgd), Jane Kelly 7 (eyeballs), Lightspring 21, 23, MoreVector
7 (heart), Opiraka 3, Petr Bonek 14, rocharibeiro 2–3, shaineast 1,
Siam Vector 18–19 (bkgd)

CONTENIDO

4

MOMIAS MISTERIOSAS

¿Qué hace que una momia sea tan horripilante? ¿Será la piel seca? ¿Los ojos sin vida? ¿O el hecho de que se trate de un cadáver de 1.000 años de antigüedad? Se han encontrado momias en todas partes del mundo. Algunas son naturales. Otras, hechas por los humanos. ¿Listo para explorar más?

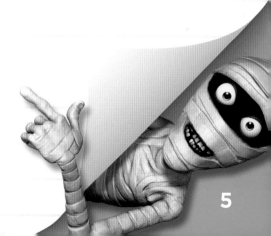

Capítulo 2
HACIENDO MOMIAS

La piel de la mayoría de los cadáveres se pudre. Se van cayendo pedazos hasta que solo queda el esqueleto. En una momia, la piel se **conserva**. A veces también lo de adentro.

Los **embalsamadores** del Antiguo Egipto secaban los cuerpos con sal. Extraían el cerebro y los órganos y los colocaban en vasijas especiales. La piel se secaba como cuero. Rellenaban las cuencas de los ojos con algodón. Luego envolvían el cuerpo con tela.

Los egipcios creían que el cuerpo momificado era el hogar del alma. Sin cuerpo, no había vida después de la muerte.

momia del pantano

momia filipina

momia inca

8

Agua, fuego y hielo

Muchas momias se han encontrado en **pantanos**. La tierra húmeda y esponjosa evita que la piel se pudra. La mayoría de los cuerpos son víctimas de asesinato. Los arrojaron a un pantano para esconder el crimen.

En Filipinas, colgaban los cuerpos por encima del fuego. El calor hacía que la piel se marchitara y se secara. ¡Todavía se pueden leer los tatuajes de sus cuerpos!

Las momias incas se encuentran en la cordillera de los Andes. El aire seco y frío las congeló. Incluso todavía tienen cabello.

Capítulo 3
MAESTROS DE LA MOMIFICACIÓN

Las momias más antiguas se encuentran en Chile. La cultura chinchorro empezó a hacer momias hace 7.000 años. Primero, les quitaban toda la piel. Luego, cortaban los músculos y los órganos. Secaban los huesos y luego volvían a armar el esqueleto. Después, estiraban la piel seca sobre los huesos. Le aplicaban a la momia una máscara de arcilla. No enterraban a la momia. Esta viajaba con su familia y celebraban juntos las festividades.

Momias modernas

Todas las momias son súper antiguas, ¿cierto? En realidad, ¡no! La tribu Anga de Papúa Nueva Guinea todavía hace momias. El cadáver desnudo se coloca elevado sobre el fuego. El calor hace que el cuerpo se **hinche**. La gente pincha el cuerpo con ramas. Los fluidos corporales salen por los agujeros. Los órganos se caen por el trasero. Cuando la piel está seca, la momia se coloca en un acantilado. Desde allí, vigila su aldea.

MOMIAS EXTRAORDINARIAS

Tutankamón, el rey de Egipto, es la momia más famosa. En 1922 encontraron su tumba inalterada. Los científicos aprendieron mucho de este descubrimiento.

El rey Tutankamón se convirtió en **faraón** a los 9 años de edad. Pero murió cuando tenía 19 años. Lo enterraron con una máscara de oro puro. En la máscara tallaron un hechizo del *Libro de los muertos*.

Su estómago, intestinos, pulmones e hígado estaban guardados en vasijas.
Su tumba estaba llena de tesoros, ropa y armas.

máscara de oro puro

Para los egipcios, los gatos eran animales sagrados. Los faraones solían ser enterrados con gatos momificados.

Ötzi

Los Alpes

Ötzi momificado

16

Ötzi, el hombre de hielo

Ötzi es una momia natural. Lo mató una flecha, en los Alpes, hace 5.300 años. Su cuerpo se congeló tan rápido que sus ojos todavía están en sus cuencas. Su cuerpo arrugado fascina a los científicos. Normalmente, un cerebro se **licúa**. Pero Ötzi todavía tiene el suyo. Está congelado dentro de su cráneo.

En el siglo XVII la gente usaba carne de momia en su medicina.

Premio a la mejor momia

¿Cuál es la momia mejor conservada jamás encontrada? ¡Lady Dai! Es una momia china de más de 2.000 años de antigüedad. Todavía tenía sangre en las venas. Su piel era suave. Tenía todo el pelo, ¡incluso en la nariz! Y los brazos y las piernas todavía podían doblarse.

Lady Dai

momia
Lady Dai

Capítulo 5

ÚNETE A LA DIVERSIÓN CON HI JINX

Las momias se ven asquerosas, pero ayudan a los científicos a comprender la historia. Puedes ver momias en los museos. ¿Quieres estudiarlas? ¡Conviértete en **arqueólogo**! Ellos estudian los objetos y cadáveres antiguos. También excavan sitios históricos. Podrías descubrir una momia antigua.

Da un paso más

1. ¿Te gustaría que te convirtieran en una momia?
   ¿Por qué sí o por qué no?

2. ¿Qué harías si encontraras una momia?

3. Investiga la vida y la religión en el antiguo Egipto. ¿En qué se diferencia de tu vida y tus creencias? ¿Es igual en algo?

GLOSARIO

arqueólogo alguien que estudia los huesos, las herramientas y la vida de los pueblos antiguos

conservar mantener vivo, intacto o libre de descomposición

embalsamador alguien que trata un cadáver con químicos especiales para evitar que se descomponga

faraón un gobernante del antiguo Egipto, como un rey o una reina

hincharse inflarse con líquido o gas

licuar convertirse en líquido

pantano una zona con tierra húmeda y suave

ÍNDICE